THE
PRANK
COOKBOOK

100 Pranks, Gags & Practical Jokes

Billy Schneider

Gottfried & Fritz

Copyright © 2015 by Gottfried & Fritz. All rights reserved.
Published in the United States
by Gottfried & Fritz, Inc., New York & Philadelphia.

www.gottfriedandfritz.com

Manufactured in the United States of America.

INTRODUCTION

The Prank Cookbook: 100 Pranks, Gags & Practical Jokes
contains 100 of the best pranks, cranks and gags. It'll tell
you exactly what you need to become a master prankster,
and the instructions are as easy as a cookbook's! Soon, you'll
be getting your parents, your friends and even your worst
enemies to fall for everything in the book! (Or, in this book
at least.)

'The Prank Cookbook' contains pranks that can be done at
home or in the office—food pranks, practical jokes and some
computer pranks too! Billy Schneider, the author, gives you
all of the ingredients and how to prepare each joke like a
meal. It's 100 different ways to prank your friends and
family! And hopefully, this book will give you all the ideas
you need for thinking of new pranks in the future too!

CONTENTS

Food Pranks

Mayonnaise Donuts	1
Chocolate-covered Brussels Sprouts	2
The Collapsing Banana	3
Water Balloon Cake	4
Orange Juice and Cheese	5
Cream Cheese Deodorant	6
Alka-Seltzer Coffee Creamer	7
Ketchup Soda	8
Jell-O Drinks	9
Solid Milk	10
Cheese Soap	11
Bowl of Reese's Pieces, M&Ms & Skittles	12
Saliva Sushi	13
Coca-Cola Mentos Explosion	14
Toothpaste Oreos	15
Frozen Breakfast Cereal	16
Chocolate-covered Eggs	17
Breaking a Finger with a Mint	18
Pregnant Turkey	19
Caramel Onions	20
Cayenne Pepper Pizza	21
Meatloaf Cake	22
Soy Sauce Soda	23

Mustard Cupcakes	24
Green Milk	25
Tabasco Brownies	26
Sunken Candy Bars	27
Chicken Bouillon Shower	28
Organic Cat Food Sandwich	29
Dog Treat Cookie Jar	30
Sugary Salt	31
Vaseline-covered Jars	32
The Old Salt Shaker Trick	33
Soap Broad	34
A Dozen Empty Eggs	35
Mustard-filled Chocolate Bunnies	36
Chalk Candies	37
Salty Sour Patch Kids	38
Spicy Reese's Peanut Butter Cups	39
Play-Doh Gum	40
Exploding Ketchup	41
Mash Potato Sundae	42
Walnut Bug Surprise	43
Sponge Brownies	44
Wasabi Guacamole	45
Plastic Hot Dog	46
Kitty Litter Cake	47
Chocolate Chip Potatoes	49
Snake in the Cereal Box	50
Hot Pepper Pranks	51
Mentos Ice	52
Eating the Uneatable	53

Disappearing Cereal	55
Don't Cry Over Spilled Milk	56
Gravy Granule Tea	57
Forgotten Milk Carton on the Car	58
Pop Rocks Alarm Clock	59

Practical Jokes

Spider in a Cup	61
Saran Wrap Clothesline	62
Broken Car Window	63
Saran Wrap on Toilet Seat	64
Soap without Suds	65
Shrunken Shoes	66
A Shower from the Sink	67
Air Unfreshener	68
Car Air Confetti-ing	69
The Fecal Prank	70
Car Whistles	71
A Numbing Brush	72
Bathroom Towel Face-Paint	73
A Yellow Flush	74
The Magic Bowl of Water Trick	75
The Immovable Sandals	77
The Fake Sneeze	78
Hair Dryer Powdering	79
The Vaseline High-Five	80
Sealing Up Tubes	81
Cockroach in the Lampshade	82

Broken Toilet Bowl	83
Glued Money	84
Short Sheet a Bed	85
Coffee Table Wake-Up	86
The Old Shaving Cream Trick	87
Quick Sand	88
Swapping Clothes	89
Air Freshener Grenade	90
Hidden Alarm Clocks	91
Locked in the Bathroom	92

Computer Pranks

Timed Shutdown	94
Broken Windows	96
Annoying Homepage	97
The Broken Mouse	99
Flipping the Landscape	100
Confusing Keys	101
Farting in Error	103
Autocorrecting Prank	105
Paint It Black	107
The Invisible Mouse	108
Task Scheduling	109
The Ever-Loading Cursor	111

FOOD PRANKS

Mayonnaise Donuts

Ingredients
6-12 donuts in a box
1 jar of mayonnaise
1 frosting tube

Find 6 to 12 glazed donuts without holes and put them in a nicely-decorated box, so that it looks like you've purchased them from a gourmet dessert shop. Fill a frosting tube with about ¼ jar of mayonnaise. Stab the frosting tube into the side of each donut and fill with mayonnaise.

When your friends go to eat the mayonnaise donuts, they will be sickened and repulsed.

Alternative Method
One can also replace the mayonnaise with ketchup to make the victim believe that they're eating a jelly donut.

Chocolate-covered Brussels Sprouts

Ingredients
12 Brussels sprouts
Chocolate fondue

Turn on the chocolate fondue and let it heat. Once the chocolate inside of the fondue has become hot and creamy, individually dip each of the 12 Brussels sprouts inside and then put them aside, letting them cool. Once the chocolate has hardened on the Brussels sprouts, place them on a dish and serve! If you're friends didn't like Brussels sprouts before, they're sure to not like them now!

The Collapsing Banana

Ingredients
1 banana
1 sewing needle

Before peeling the banana, take your sewing needle and carve small, hairline-sized cuts into the side of the banana peel, slicing the banana. Once done, leave in the pile of bananas and serve. When someone goes to peel the banana and open it, it will collapse and break into small pieces, falling all over the floor!

Water Balloon Cake

Ingredients
1 water balloon
1 bottle of water
1 canister of icing
1 chocolate cake

Scoop the center out of a chocolate cake, so that there is a wide-open crater in the center. Fill one water balloon with water. Place the water balloon in the center of the cake and then generously cover both the cake and the water balloon in icing. When someone goes to cut the cake, they'll be in for a shocking burst!

Orange Juice and Cheese

Ingredients
1 bottle with a lid
1 glass of orange juice or Sunny Delight
1 packet of powdered cheese (ideally from Kraft macaroni and cheese)

Pour 1 glass of orange juice or Sunny Delight in a bottle with a lid. Add ¼ powdered cheese from macaroni and cheese package and then close the lid on the bottle. Shake it up for a moment until the powdered cheese and orange juice has mixed. Serve either in the bottle or, for more effectiveness, pour the mixture in a glass and serve. Ensured to disgust family and friends!

Cream Cheese Deodorant

Ingredients
1 stick of deodorant
1 stick of cream cheese
1 tablespoon
1 butter knife

Remove the cap from the stick of deodorant. Use your butter knife to cut off the top of the stick. Take one clump of cream cheese using your spoon and place it on the top of the deodorant stick. (Be sure to make the top of the deodorant in an arc-shape so that it's convincing to whoever's going to be using it.) Place the lid back on and dispose of the portion of deodorant that you've cut off. Served in the morning, after your friends shower, and sure to make whoever's going to be using this deodorant smell like a festering bowl of old cheese all day! Yum!

Alka-Seltzer Coffee Creamer

Ingredients
1 box of Alka-Seltzer pills
1 Coffee-mate powdered coffee creamer
1 cup of coffee
1 hammer

Remove the cap from the Coffee-mate coffee creamer and dump the contents into the waste-bin. Place the entire box of Alka-Seltzer pills into a small Tupperware container and crush them up with your hammer. Once the Alka-Seltzer pills are ground down into a dust, pour the contents into the emptied Coffee-mate container and seal the lid. When your friend or loved one goes to pour the Coffee-mate creamer into their coffee that morning, the cup will explode in front of them! You don't need to worry about them actually drinking it, because the coffee will be all over the kitchen floor!

Ketchup Soda

Ingredients
1 disposable soda cup with lid
1 straw
1 small cup of ketchup

Remove the lid from the empty disposal cup and then place the smaller cup of ketchup inside of the cup. Place the bottom of the straw into the center of the ketchup cup and then place the lid back on. When someone goes to take a sip of this drink, he or she will be sure to taste nothing but a tomato-based sauce.

Jell-O Drinks

Ingredients
glass cup
plastic straw
Jell-O

Make Jell-O as you normally would, but, instead of putting it in a small dish, pour the mix into a drinking glass. Make sure the glass is one that you'd normally drink from and then insert the straw in the center of the mold. (Be sure to put the straw in the mold before it hardens, not afterwards.)

Once the Jell-O has hardened, serve it to one of your family members or friends on a hot summer's day. When they go to sip from the straw, they'll find it impossible to break through the Jell-O!

Solid Milk

Ingredients
1 tall glass of milk
1 cup of gelatin
2 cookies

Pour milk into a glass. Pour gelatin into the milk and then mix them together. Place the mixture into the refrigerator and let sit for about one hour.

Once done, remove the glass and serve. When your friends and family go to sip this refreshing glass of milk, they'll find that it's as hard as stone. And better yet, when they go to dip their cookie into the rock-hard milk, the cookie will almost break. Cheers!

Cheese Soap

Ingredients
1 slice of gourmet cheese
1 bar of soap

The health-food craze is not the only thing that's popular these days; people are also into organic toothpastes, hair products and even soap bars. If a friend of yours has recently purchased one of those fancy soap bars, then it'd be the prime time to swap it out with a festering chunk of cheese.

Remove soap bar from friend's soap tray. Slice one piece of gourmet cheese resembling soap bar into a shape that resembles the soap. Swap out soap bar for soap and wait for friend or family member to shower the following morning. Their friends and co-workers will ask that morning, "Who cut the cheese?"

Bowl of Reese's Pieces, M&M & Skittles

Ingredients
1 bag of M&Ms
1 bag of Skittles
1 bag of Reese's Pieces
1 bowl

Remove M&M, Skittles and Reese's Pieces candies from the bags and pour them into a large bowl. Mix the candies around in the bowl and serve. When someone comes around to dig into this mixture of sweet, peanut-buttery chocolate, they'll be sure to cringe! Bon appétit!

Saliva Sushi

Ingredients
1 roll of sushi
1 piece of seaweed

Place a roll of your favorite sushi on a dish and serve to your friend. Be sure to tell them that you prepared the sushi yourself. Once your friend takes the first bite and tells them that it's delicious, ask them if they want another roll. When they consent, start to lick a piece of seaweed with a straight face and watch their reaction as your prepare your saliva-covered sushi. It'll leave your friend saying, no, domo arigato!

Coca-Cola Mentos Explosion

Ingredients
1 bottle of Coca-Cola
1 Mentos mint
1 sewing needle
1 piece of dental floss.

Feed one piece of dental floss into the eye of a needle and then stab the Mentos mint with the needle, feeding the dental floss completely through. The mint should have about 1 to 2 inches of dental floss coming out of both sides. Uncap the bottle of Coca-Cola and place the mint on the inside of the cap. Place the cap back on, but allow the two pieces of dental floss to hang out of both sides of the cap (so that the mint doesn't fall in and make a mess— for you!) Once the cap is back on, the two pieces of dental floss should be hanging out of the sides of the cap. Snip them both with a scissor, so that your friend doesn't notice that something's awry. Serve.

Once your friend opens the bottle, the mint will fall in and the soda will explode. Ka-boom!

Toothpaste Oreos

Ingredients
A sleeve of Oreo cookies
1 butter knife
1 tube of toothpaste

Remove Oreo cookies from the sleeve and then gently separate the two chocolate cookies. Scrape the sugary glaze off the separated cookies and then place the cookies flat on your kitchen table. Put a small amount of toothpaste on the cleared-off chocolate cookie and then shut it tight like a sandwich. When someone goes to bite into the cookie, they will find themselves feeling a minty and refreshing taste in their mouth.

Frozen Breakfast Cereal

Ingredients
1 bowl
1 spoon
1 box of cereal
1 cup of milk

Pour breakfast cereal of your choice and milk into a small bowl. Place the spoon into the bowl as you would if you were to eat the bowl of cereal, then place the entire bowl into the freezer for one hour.

Once the bowl has frozen, remove from the refrigerator and serve. When someone goes to live up the spoon, they'll find that the entire bowl goes up with it!

Chocolate-covered Eggs

Ingredients
1 raw egg
chocolate fondue
aluminum foil

Carefully dip one raw egg in chocolate fondue.
Place the egg on a paper towel and let sit so that the
chocolate dries. Cover the egg in a colorful
aluminum plastic wrapping and serve. The crunch
will be most egg-cellent!

Breaking a Finger with a Mint

Ingredients
1 hard mint
1 finger
Acting skills

When you're out at dinner with some friends, place a mint in your mouth without anyone knowing. Start to bite on your nail and then complain that something's lodged in the back of your tooth. Stick your finger half-way into your mouth and, when it's there, crunch down on the mint and scream. But be sure to tell your friends its all a prank before the ambulance comes!

Pregnant Turkey

Ingredients
1 large turkey
1 Cornish hen

While you're stuffing your turkey this Thanksgiving, add a Cornish hen in with the traditional stuffing and cook as you normally would. Hand the knife to one of your family members and tell them to take out the stuffing. To their astonishment, a Cornish hen—or a smaller turkey—will be inside. Just tell them it's a pregnant turkey, even though we all know that birds lay eggs!

Caramel Onions

Ingredients
Caramel fondue
6 onions
6 wooden sticks

Caramel apples are a popular treat for many people but, today, we're going to learn how to make caramel onions.

Stick wooden stick into the center of the onion. Dip onions into caramel fondue and put aside until dry. Once dried, serve caramel onions to friends and family. It's a treat so delicious that whoever eats it will cry with delight!

Cayenne Pepper Pizza

Ingredients
1 cheese pizza
1 bag of powdered cayenne pepper

Take one pizza pie and let it cool. Once it has cooled, gently lift the cheese off one of the slices. Take 1 tablespoon of powdered cayenne pepper and sprinkle generously over the slice. Once done, place the cheese back down onto the slice and pat it down gently.

(Caution! Do not do this prank to someone who might either be allergic or sensitive to cayenne pepper. The results can be maddening!)

Meatloaf Cake

Ingredients
1 meatloaf
1 cup of icing

Cook meatloaf in the oven as you normally would. Let the meatloaf cool and put it on a dish. Spread the entire meatloaf in the icing, allowing none of the meat to be exposed. Let it sit again and serve. Your friends and family will be sure to spit out your delicious cake of meat! Mm-mm!

Soy Sauce Soda

Ingredients
1 bottle of soy sauce
1 bottle of Sprite
1 bottle of Coca-Cola

Open bottle of Coca-Cola and dump contents into the sink. Open bottle of Sprite and dump 1/2 of the contents into the empty bottle of Coca-Cola. Then, continue to pour soy sauce into the Sprite (which is now in the Coca-Cola bottle) until the color becomes brown, much like that of Coca-Cola, and serve. Delicious!

Mustard Cupcakes

Ingredients
6 cupcakes
1 bottle of mustard

Make cupcakes as you normally would but, instead of adding frosting on the top, craftily pour mustard on top. If friends ask about the yellow frosting, just tell them that it's food coloring and, as they go into take a bite, they'll be served the most bitter cupcakes they've ever tasted. Yuck!

Green Milk

Ingredients
1 gallon of milk
1 packet of food coloring

Remove the cap from the gallon of milk and pour food coloring into the gallon. Shake up the mixture until the milk becomes a solid green color. Place back in the refrigerator and await the reaction of your friends and family!

Tabasco Brownies

Ingredients
1 plate of brownies
1 bottle of Tabasco sauce

Prepare a dish of brownies as you normally would. Once laid out on a nice, appealing dish, splash some Tabasco sauce onto the top. Because of the brownies' dark, chocolatey surface, no one will ever notice—until they've taken a bite! Mama mia!

Sunken Candy Bars

Ingredients
1 Snickers candy bar
1 swimming pool

On a hot summer's day at the pool, remove one Snickers bar from its packaging and place it in the pocket of your swim trunks. Drop the candy bar in the center of the pool when no one is looking and let it sit. Once done, scream, "There's doodie in the pool!" and watch as the entire pool evacuates for fear of water-born diseases.

Chicken Bouillon Shower

Ingredients
1 shower-head
6 cubes of chicken bouillon

Twist off the shower head in your shower. Remove the chicken bouillon from package and stuff into the bottom of the shower-head. Twist shower-head back onto the shower head and run water to make sure that it is working properly. If you smell a chicken-scented water, then you can be sure that the prank is working as planned. Once done, wait until your friend or family member takes a shower and goes to work smelling like freshly-cooked chicken.

Organic Cat Food Sandwich

Ingredients
1 canister of cat food
2 slices of bread

Since everyone these days seem to be so interested in eating healthy, the organic cat food sandwich prank has come just in time for this health-food craze.

Purchase one canister of cat food from your local grocery store. Once home, spread it generously over a slice of bread and place the other slice atop it, forming a sandwich. Make a traditional tuna sandwich for yourself.

Once your friend or family member comes into the room, tell them that you've made them a sandwich. When you're eating yours, show the person how much you're enjoying yours and then ask how delicious the organic sandwiches are. You'll be surprised by their response! And then you can tell them, once and for all, that theirs is "organic cat food."

Dog Treat Cookie Jar

Ingredients
1 cookie jar
1 bag of dog treats

For this prank, be sure to acquire a bag of dog treats that are not shaped like bones or something else that will make them look like dog treats. Purchase one of the new, inconspicuous dog treats that can easily be confused for standard cookies. Once done, dump the entire bag into a cookie jar and serve! Your friends will bark with anger!

Sugary Salt

Ingredients
1 bag of sugar
1 salt shaker

Remove the salt from a salt shaker. Pour sugar in the salt shaker and then wait for a friend to sprinkle it generously on his or her favorite soup or meat. It'll be the sweetest seasoning that anyone has ever had!

Vaseline–covered Jars

Ingredients
1 canister of Vaseline
1 difficult-to-open jar

Find a difficult-to-open jar, such as a jar of olives or meat sauce. Spread some Vaseline on the sides of the lid—but not too generously. Then hand the jar to a friend and ask him or her to open it. You'll watch them struggle for several minutes and get a good laugh, but be sure to tell your friend it's all a prank before they burst a blood vessel!

Rinse the Vaseline after the jar afterwards and enjoy your olives or meat sauce with your friend or family member.

The Old Salt Shaker Prank

Ingredients
1 salt shaker

A prank as old as time, the Old Salt Shaker Prank is still guaranteed to work and to trap anyone in its snare.

Loosen the cap of a salt shaker and wait. When an unsuspecting victim comes around to turn the salt shaker over and season their dish, the entire salt shaker will pour out onto their dish, forming a small dune of salt. A classic, but sure to get 'em every time!

Soap Bread

Ingredients
1 bar of soap
1 microwave

Place bar of soap into a traditional microwave and set the timer for 1 minute. The soap will turn into something that resembles a freshly-toasted bun. Place bun onto a dish and serve. It'll wash out your friend's dirty mouth in no time!

A Dozen Empty Eggs

Ingredients
1 dozen eggs
1 nail

Gently bore the tip of a small nail into a raw egg, but be sure not to crack the egg. Once the nail is in the egg, twist and turn the nail around so that the yolk inside is broken up. Once done, bore another hole into the bottom of the egg and continue to rock the nail back and forth. Finally, place the opening of a straw on one of the holes and start to blow. The yolk will soon come out of the other side, emptying the entire egg of its yolk.

A number of pranks can be done with emptied eggs, such as dropping one in front of a friend or throwing one at someone all of a sudden. It'll surely be time consuming to make a dozen of these eggs, but use your imagination and think about the possibilities with emptied eggs!

Mustard-filled Chocolate Bunnies

Ingredients
1 chocolate bunny
1 bottle of mustard
1 icing tube

Gently remove the aluminum wrapper from the chocolate bunny. Bore a small hole in the bottom of the chocolate bunny with a large nail. Fill an icing tube with mustard and inject the mustard into the chocolate bunny. Rewrap the bunny, but make sure that it's going to look convincing.

Once done, serve the bunny to a friend and watch as the mustard bursts out of the Easter treat! Yum!

Chalk Candies

Ingredients
1 piece of chalk
1 aluminum wrapper

Go to a local toy store and search for a piece of side walk chalk that is in the shape of a farm animal or something else that might resemble a piece of Easter candy. Wrap the side walk chalk in a piece of colorful aluminum. Serve to a friend or family member and watch as they devour the chalky goodness! Delicious!

Salty Sour Patch Kids

Ingredients
1 bag of Sour Patch Kids
1 salt shaker
1 spray bottle

Remove some Sour Patch Kids out of the bag and lay them down on a paper towel. Spray them lightly with some water and then shake some salt on top of them. Place the Sour Patch Kids back into the bag and serve. If you can't begin to think what it'll taste like, just wait for your friends reaction and laugh!

Spicy Reese's Peanut Butter Cups

Ingredients
1 Reese's peanut butter cup
1 bottle of Sriracha hot sauce

Gently remove the paper from the bottom of a Reese's peanut butter cup and flip the chocolate over. Bore a small hole in the bottom, but make sure to keep a piece of chocolate to cover the hole back up later. Then, pour some Sriracha hot sauce into the hole made on the bottom of the Reese's peanut butter cup. Gently cover the hole with a piece of chocolate and then firmly place the wrapper back on. Serve and watch your friends run for the sink!

Play–Doh Gum

Ingredients
1 box of gum
1 cup of Play-Doh

Find an appropriately-colored Play-Doh that will match the color of the gum you've selected. If it's a mint Orbit gum, then purchase a green or blue Play-Doh. If it's hot peppermint, then purchase a red-colored Play-Doh and so on. Then, unwrap the individual pieces of gum and mold the Play-Doh in the shape of them gum. Cover the gum-shaped Play-Doh in the wrapper and place it back in the gum box. Serve to friends or co-workers, or anyone who asks for gum. They'll never bother you again!

Exploding Ketchup

Ingredients
1 half-filled bottle of ketchup
1 box of baking soda

Turn over a half-filled bottle of ketchup and allow the bottle to sit until all of the ketchup has run down the insides of the bottle and reached the cap. Once the inside of the bottle is completely covered in ketchup and all of the glass looks red, turn it over, remove the cap and put a tablespoon of baking soda inside. DO NOT SHAKE. Put the cap back on and then place it in the refrigerator to serve.

The moment that a friend goes into the refrigerator and shakes the bottle, the ketchup will explode all over the kitchen, causing quite a mess!

Mashed Potato Sundae

Ingredients
1 bowl of mashed potatoes
1 cup of gravy
1 ice cream sundae glass
1 cherry
1 ice cream scooper

Use an ice cream scooper to scoop out mashed potatoes and put into a ice cream sundae glass. Once the glass is full of mashed potatoes, pour some gravy on top and then add a cherry for good measure. Serve and tell your friend that it's the best ice cream sundae you've ever had!

Walnut Bug Surprise

Ingredients
1 walnut
1 dead insect
super glue

Carefully crack the shell of a walnut and remove the contents from the inside. Place some dead insects inside of the walnut and then super-glue it back together. When your friend or family member goes to open it, they'll be more than surprised!

(The bugs can also be replaced with small trinkets or candies for a more harmless prank.)

Sponge Brownies

Ingredients
1 kitchen sponge
chocolate icing

Take a small sponge from your kitchen and generously spread chocolate icing all over it. Put some sprinkles on top as well to make it look more appealing and serve. It'll be the roughest brownie your friend has ever tasted!

Wasabi Guacamole

Ingredients
1 bottle of wasabi
1 bowl of guacamole

Generously pour one bottle of wasabi into a bowl of guacamole and mix. Since the both are green in color, it'll remain inconspicuous and your friends will never notice—until they eat that first nacho!

Plastic Hot Dog

Ingredients
1 plastic hot dog
1 hot dog bun
relish
ketchup
mustard

Place one plastic hot dog in a hot dog bun. Cover with the condiments of your choice and wait to see your friend's reaction as he takes the first bite! The more condiments, the better, however, since it will conceal the plastic hot dog.

Kitty Litter Cake

Ingredients
1 box spice or German chocolate cake mix
1 box of white cake mix
1 package white sandwich cookies
1 large package vanilla instant pudding mix
Some drops of green food coloring
12 small Tootsie Rolls
1 new cat litter box
1 new cat litter box liner
1 new pooper scooper

Make the chocolate and white cake mixes as the sides of the packages direct you to do. Blend or crumble the cookies so as to make them as alike to kitty litter as possible. Put some green food coloring to 1 cup of the cookie crumbs and shake it around in a jar, then set aside.

Once the cakes have reached room temperature, crumble them into a bowl. Toss half of the cookie crumbs remaining and some pudding into a mixture, but make sure that it doesn't get too soggy. Place some liner in the litter box and pour the mixture in.

Place the Tootsie rolls in a microwave until soft. Shape the ends into slightly curved points, so that they resemble cat feces. Scatter the Tootsie rolls throughout the cake mixture and sprinkle the remaining white cookie crumbs over the mixture, scattering green crumbs lightly on top.

Finally, put your kitty litter box on a piece of newspaper and shove the pooper scooper in. And to shock your friends and family, start eating from the cake when they enter the room. But be sure to tell them it's a prank before they make a phone call to the insane asylum! Bon appétit!

Chocolate Chip Potatoes

Ingredients
1 container of mashed potatoes
1 cup of black beans

Mix the mashed potatoes and the black beans in bowl. Lay out portions of the mixture on a baking sheet, as if they were chocolate chip cookies. Bake at 350°F until the potatoes are golden brown (approximately 20 minutes). Serve and tell your friends that they're the best chocolate chip cookies you've ever had! And when the joke's all over, you'll still have some good potatoes to eat! Even bring out some salsa!

Snake in the Cereal Box

Ingredients
1 plastic snake
1 box of cereal

Bury the snake in the cereal box. Close the box up securely and wait for an unsuspecting friend or family member to pour their cereal in the morning. It'll be a sneaky and snake-like thing to do, but it'll at least amount to a laugh or two for everyone involved!

Hot Pepper Pranks

Ingredients
1 pepper

The Trinidad Scorpion Butch T, the Trinidad Moruga Scorpion and the Carolina Reaper are said to be some of the hottest peppers in the world. But if you're not looking to kill your friends and family, I'd suggest a more mild pepper for any of the following pepper-related pranks. The habanero is usually a more sensible option.

Here are some pranks to use with the habanero.

1. Mix one hot habanero pepper in with a pile of peppers. Eat some of the standard chile peppers yourself and then hand one of the habaneros that you've mixed in the batch to one of your friends or family members.

2. Slip the habanero in one of your loved one's dishes. The habanero can be hid beneath slices of pizza and in more elaborate Indian and Mexican dishes.

Mentos Ice

Ingredients
1 cup of Coca-Cola
1 package of Mentos mints
ice tray

Fill all of the cells on an ice tray with water. Place a Mentos mint in each of the cells. Place in freezer and let sit for 2 hours or until frozen. Once done, place ice cubs in a friend's Coca-Cola. The moment that the ice thaws out, the Mentos will be released into the Coca-Cola and cause an explosion that will be leaving him sticky and completely confused!

Eating the Uneatable

Since this prank, "Eating the Uneatable," comes in many forms and can be modified even further, I'm going to list the several different ways in which can be done. This prank is basically removing the contents from the container of something that is normally poisonous or disgusting and replacing it with something more wholesome.

In order to implement this prank, the prankster will need to be acting as if he is actually enjoying the contents of whatever he's consuming, and will have to implement this prank in front of friends and/or family.

1. **Water in a vodka bottle**. Remove the contents from a bottle of vodka. Pour water into the bottle. Consume in front of friends, causing them to think that you're drinking yourself almost to death.

2. **Gatorade in a surface cleaner bottle**. Remove contents from surface cleaner bottle, such as Windex, and clean out the container well. Replace the contents with whichever Gatorade flavor

matches the contents of the cleaner and, when a friend or family member walks in, uncap the surface cleaner bottle and begin to drink. Delicious!

3. **Vanilla pudding in mayonnaise**. Remove the contents from a mayonnaise jar and replace them with vanilla pudding. Consume in front of friends.

4. **Grape juice in Listerine bottle**. Remove the contents of a purple-colored Listerine bottle and fill it with grape juice. Take a small swig of the Listerine and then proceed to drink the entire bottle, causing consternation amongst your loved ones.

Disappearing Cereal

Ingredients
1 box of cereal
1 pair of scissors

Remove bag from the cereal box. Cut a large hole on the bottom of the cereal box with your scissors. Place the cereal box on the counter top, but do not remove the box from its position. Dump the contents of the bag into the box and close it up. Let sit.

When your friend or family member comes into the kitchen in the morning to pour their cereal, they'll be welcomed by little remnants of their precious breakfast cereal scattered all over the kitchen! And it will all disappear from the box! Violà!

Don't Cry Over Spilled Milk

Ingredients
1 gallon of milk
1 box cutter

Pour the contents of a milk gallon into a bowl. Either dump the contents or save. Ensure that only 1/2 of the milk gallon is full. Look closely at the milk gallon and search for a line down the center. Carefully cut down this small line with your blade and then place the milk gallon back into the refrigerator and let sit. When your victim comes to pour their morning bowl of cereal, they'll cause the milk to pour all over the counter top! But when they complain, just tell them not to cry over spilled milk!

Gravy Granule Tea

Ingredients
1 tea bag
1 canister of gravy granules
sharp knife
sellotape

Slice a small slit in the top of the teabag with your knife. Pour out the contents of the teabag. Take a teaspoon of the gravy granules and place as much as possible in the teabag. Once full, seal the teabag with some sellotape.

When a friend comes over for tea, be sure to offer him one of the gravy granule teas to steep in his cup of hot water. He'll likely not finish the whole cup, but the first sip is enough to make this prank worth it!

Forgotten Milk Carton on the Car

Ingredients
1 milk carton
2 maximum strength magnets
1 car

Pour out the contents of the milk carton. Place a maximum strength magnet inside the emptied milk carton. Once done, place the milk carton on the roof of the car and then, place the second magnet on the inside of the car roof, so that the two magnets can attract and keep the carton in place. Drive away, but don't head into onto a highway! Drive into a town center or a supermarket parking lot, where there are enough people around to notice the prank, but where you're not going so fast that the carton flies off!

Pop-rocks Alarm Clock

Ingredients
1 bag of Pop-rocks

Should you find a friend or family member sleeping in the living room with their mouth open, it might be time to implement the Pop-rocks Alarm Clock Prank.

Open the bag of pop-rocks. Gently place some of them in the mouth of your sleeping friend or family member and wait to see the expression on their face as they wake up with a strange crackling in their mouth!

PRACTICAL JOKES

Spider in a Cup

Ingredients
1 plastic spider
1 clear plastic cup
1 piece of cardboard

Place the plastic spider in the cup. Cover the plastic cup with the piece of cardboard and hold it tight, pretending that you managed to catch the insect. Once done, call your friends and/or family into the room, quickly show them the insect and then drop the cup, pretending that it was an accident. It'll be sure to give you a good laugh or two, but you'll likely be laughing alone, as everyone else will be long gone!

Saran Wrap Clothesline

Ingredients
1 roll of saran wrap
1 door

Securely place a piece of saran wrap on a door in your house, school or workplace. Cause someone else to run after you or to just run into the room. Once done, duck beneath the saran wrap and turn around, so that you can see your friend or family member run face-first into the saran wrap on the door.

Broken Car Window

Ingredients
1 gardening tool with a long handle
1 piece of glass
1 car

In order for this prank to work properly, the prankster needs to make sure that his victim's car is in a garage. If it is, he must first roll down the window of the car and then place a gardening tool in the window (so as to make it look as if it had fallen onto the car). Once done, place pieces of broken glass at the bottom of the car, so as to make it look that the car window has smashed. In the morning, your friend or loved one will be screaming with their hands on their head, but, once they know it's all a prank, they'll love you and feel relieved.

Caution: This prank involves broken glass and the necessary precautions should be taken to ensure that the prankster does not incur injury, from either the glass or his victims.

Saran Wrap on Toilet Seat

Ingredients
1 roll of saran wrap
1 toilet

Lift the toilet seat. Securely tighten one strip of saran wrap over the toilet bowl and then place down the toilet seat. (If the saran wrap is placed directly on the seat, this prank will be ineffective.) Finally, wait for your friend or family member to relieve themselves in the morning and patiently wait to hear their frustration from the other room. Just make sure that they clean it all up in the end!

Soap without Suds

Ingredients
1 bar of soap
1 bottle of nail polish

Place one bar of soap on a paper towel. Gently cover the entire bar in the nail polish with a brush. Let the bar sit for about an hour until the polish has dried completely. Once done, place it back in the shower and wait for someone to use the soap, which won't lather. This prank will cause as much confusion for the victim as it will laughter for the prankster!

Shrunken Shoes

Ingredients
1 pair of shoes
1 bag of cotton balls

Remove cotton balls from the bag. Stuff them tightly into the toes of your friend or family member's shoes. When they go to put on their shoes, they'll quickly think that their feet have either grown smaller or something is wrong with their shoes. Just watch in the distance as the victim struggles to think which one is the case.

A Shower from the Sink

Ingredients
1 strip of duct tape

Take one strip of duct tape and cover it over a faucet. Be sure to leave a small gap in the duct tape so that when the person standing in front of it turns it on, they'll be in store for an unexpected shower!

This prank is an old one, but is always guaranteed to make for some good laughs!

Alternative Method
One can replace the strip of tape with a rubber band for similar results.

Air Unfreshener

Ingredients
1 spray can of bait spray
1 spray can of air freshener

Carefully remove the plastic label and secure cap covering the top of the aerosol air freshener. Wrap the plastic label of the air freshener around the bait spray can and plastic the secure cap on top as well.

Car Air Confetti-ing

Ingredients
small strips of paper (or confetti)
1 car air-condition system

Create or purchase small strips of confetti (small hole punches will also do). Carefully place the confetti in the air conditioning vents on a friend's car. Be patient.

Once your friend turns on his car's air conditioning, the confetti will spray all throughout the car and the laugh will be one worth celebrating!

A Fecal Prank

Ingredients
1 toilet paper roll

Remove the toilet paper from a toilet paper roll and set aside the cardboard tube inside (or just take a cardboard tube from a toilet paper roll if you have one set aside already for some reason). Rinse the cardboard tube in lukewarm water until completely wet. Tear the wet tube into inch to two-inch long pieces. Tightly squeeze the pieces of wet cardboard in your hand and open your hand. The result will be something that resembles feces.

Once done, place the feces wherever you think suitable. It can be placed on the toilet seat, on the floor of the bathroom or even somewhere in the kitchen. Although it might be shocking at first glance, it'll be safe, since it's only cardboard!

Car Whistles

Safe Method – Ingredients
Ingredients (Method 2)
1 harmonica
1 roll of duct tape

Place harmonica onto the grill of your friend's car and let it sit. Once your friend begins to drive, he will hear something strange coming from his engine. It might take him quite a while to discover the harmonica, but when he does, he'll recall that the strange noise was in the key of G the whole time.

Less Safe Method – Ingredients
1 roll of duct tape
1 whistle

Cover the muffler of a car in strips of duct tape. Cut a small opening on the duct tape covering the muffler. Place a small whistle in the opening and let sit. When your friend begins to drive, he'll notice that a whistling sound is coming from his car—and the faster he goes, the louder the whistle gets.

A Numbing Brush

Ingredients
1 tube of toothpaste
1 tube of maximum strength Orajel

Squeeze the toothpaste out of an entire tube of toothpaste. Place the small nozzle of the maximum strength Orajel into the toothpaste tube and push. Make sure that the entire bottle of Orajel has been transferred to the toothpaste and then wait. Your friend will be in store for a numbing morning brush!

Bathroom Towel Face-Paint

Ingredients
1 towel
1 package of food coloring

Purchase a food coloring and colored towel that match. That means, if the towel is green, then purchase green food coloring. Cover the towel in the food coloring, but make sure that it isn't too conspicuous. Let sit and wait for friend to come out of the shower and dry himself off. He will soon find that he's green with envy at his not having thought of the idea!

A Yellow Flush

Ingredients
1 package of yellow food coloring
1 toilet

Remove lid from toilet bowl tank. Pour one package of yellow food coloring into the toilet bowl tank. Let sit.

When a friend or family member flushes the toilet, he or she will think that the pipes are broken. It will seem that the toilet is flushing, but that urine won't go down. Be sure to tell them it's a prank before a plumber comes in!

Alternative Method
Another method of this prank would be to place red food coloring in the toilet bowl tank, so that your victim thinks its blood. But such a prank should be done with caution and not to those who are queasy or easily faint from the sight of blood.

The Magic Bowl of Water Trick

Ingredients
1 bowl of water
1 chair
1 long stick

This one is a bit difficult to implement, as the victim needs to be entirely gullible. But have faith and it should serve for a great laugh!

Place a long stick somewhere in the premises. Fill a large bowl with water. Set up a chair in the middle of the kitchen or living room (ideally in the kitchen, since you don't want your entire carpet getting wet).

Stand on the chair, hold the bowl of water securely against the ceiling. Call your friend or loved one into the room while you're standing on the chair and holding the bowl of water against the ceiling. Tell the person that you want to show them a "magic trick," and that you will "make the bowl disappear." All that they need to do is to pick up the stick and to apply pressure to the bowl which you're holding against the ceiling. Once you're convinced that the person is holding the bowl securely against the ceiling with the stick, quickly let go of the bowl, jump off the chair and take it away, leaving your victim all alone.

The only escape for them is to get entirely wet or for you, the prankster, to have some pity on them. But let the prank ride out and laugh!

The Immovable Sandals

Ingredients
1 pair of sandals
1 tube of super glue

Place the sandals or shoes of a loved one in the garage or on a surface that you don't mind getting too damaged. Flip them over so that the soles of the shoes or sandals are facing you and cover them entirely in super glue. Turn the sandals over and place them securely on the ground. Let sit for about 1 hour.

When your friend or family member goes to put their feet in their shoes, they'll find that they're entirely immovable! They might even stick their feet into them quickly and fall on the ground, creating the most laughter that this prank can possibly create! Enjoy!

The Fake Sneeze

Ingredients
1 handful of water

Cup a handful of lukewarm water. Step behind one of your friends or family members and both gently splash the water on their neck and pretend to sneeze. They'll turn around and wipe their neck looking angry, thinking that you've covered them with snot. But rest assured, once they know that it's just water, they'll calm down, but will nonetheless call you a fool!

Hair Dryer Powdering

Ingredients
1 hair dryer
1 bottle of talcum (baby) powder

Twist open the cap on a bottle of baby powder. Unplug the hair dryer and turn it so that the opening is facing you. Generously pour some of the baby powder into the opening, but be careful not to spill it all over the counter top. Place the hair dryer down gently so that no one notices that it's been tampered with. Plug the hair dryer back into the outlet and tilt it on it's side, so that it looks that someone's just left it there.

When your sister or mother goes to turn on the hair dryer, they'll be welcomed with some powder in their powder room! Ha!

The Vaseline High–Five

Ingredients
1 container of Vaseline
2 hands

Generously cover the palm of your hand in Vaseline. Approach a friend or family member and joyously hold out your hand, saying, "High five!" When your victim slaps your hand, they'll feel a viscous wetness on theirs. Just reassure them and tell them that it's Vaseline once you've had yourself a good laugh!

Sealing Up Tubes

Ingredients
1 tube of any personal care product
1 strip of saran wrap

Choose a tube of toothpaste, body wash, shampoo, or anything that someone would use for personal care. Remove the cap from the tube. Take a small strip of saran wrap (possibly about the size of a dime) and secure it tightly over the mouth of the tube. Place the cap back on the tube and tighten it.

When someone goes into the bathroom to brush their teeth, wash their hair or clean themselves, they'll be confused as to why the tube feels full but nothing is coming out. They'll poke and prod until they've realized that someone has tampered with their tube!

Cockroach in the Lampshade

Ingredients
1 plastic cockroach
1 lampshade
1 strip of duct tape

Turn off the lamp. Roll up a small strip of duct tape or electrical tape. Place it securely on the underbelly of the plastic cockroach. Reach your hand into the lampshade and adhere the plastic cockroach to the inner portion of the lampshade. Turn on the lamp to test the prank and to see if the shadow of the cockroach will appear in the lampshade. If done correctly, let sit and wait for your victim to go to bed. It'll probably bug whoever you're doing this do, but it'll all be worth it for a laugh!

Broken Toilet Bowl

Ingredients
1 small bag of uncooked macaroni
1 toilet bowl

Lift up the seat of the toilet. Carefully place a bag of uncooked macaroni on the lip of the toilet bowl (with the seat lifted up), but make sure that it's small enough so that none of the bag is hanging over the edge. Carefully place the toilet bowl seat back down on the bag of macaroni and let it sit.

When someone comes in to plop down on the toilet, they'll hear a sudden crunch and think that they've broken the toilet seat. It'll send them flying off with their pants down!

Glued Money

Ingredients
1 tube of super glue
1 dollar bill, credit card or coin

Find a crowded street somewhere in town. Remove the cap from your tube of super glue and squeeze the glue generously on the back of a coin, a dollar bill or a credit card. Adhere the object firmly on the side walk and then take a seat.

When people come by and notice the object, they'll reach down and attempt to pick it up. They might struggle for a minute before realizing that it's glued to the ground but, in the meantime, you'll be watching and laughing from a safe distance. Enjoy!

Short Sheet a Bed

Ingredients
1 bed
2 sheets

This is a classic prank that grandmothers and mothers have been playing on their kids for years, but it can be difficult to describe, so read closely.

Remove the comforter entirely from the bed. Make sure that the bed sheets with the elastic in the edges and the loose bed sheets are both the same color. Cover the mattress in the bed sheets without the elastic and tuck it tightly beneath the mattress near the headboard. Walk over the foot of the bed and fold the sheet up near the headboard. The illusion that you're trying to create is to have the BOTTOM of the bed sheets (the part that you've folded) look like it's the folded portion on the top of the bed sheets. Place the comforter back on the bed.

Once done, someone will attempt to lift the sheets and leap into bed—but that won't work.

Coffee-Table Wake up

Ingredients
1 coffee table
1 sleeping friend
1 pot
1 spoon

In order for this prank to work properly, you need to find a friend sleeping on the floor. (However, I'm sure that someone can manage an alternative version with someone sleeping in the bed.)

Find a friend sleeping on the floor. Place a short coffee table over the friend's head. Once done, lift up your pot and spoon and begin to slam them together as violently as you can. The noise will cause your friend to lunge up out of his sleep, smacking his head on the coffee table.

Caution: Don't use a glass coffee table, as this might cause a much more dangerous alternative of the prank.

The Old Shaving Cream Trick

Ingredients
1 canister of shaving cream
1 feather or piece of yarn

Much like the Old Salt Shaker Prank, the Old Shaving Cream Prank is as old as time.

Find a sleeping friend or family member. Cover his or her palm in a generous amount of shaving cream. Do not laugh. Take your feather (or piece of yarn) and use it to lightly tickle his or her nose. The victim will likely go to scratch their nose and will, in turn, slap a handful of shaving cream on their own face.

Once again, it's an old one, but one that never fails! Hand them a razor and some warm water if you don't want to waste the shaving cream. Might as well shave while they have the chance!

Quick Sand

Ingredients
1 shovel
1 beach towel

This prank is one that can only be implemented in the summertime when you and a friend are at the beach.

When your friend is gone, use your shovel to dig a deep hole in the sand. Once done, carefully place your friend's beach towel over the trench (but make sure that the hole isn't larger than the towel, as this will surely give it away).

Be clam and don't laugh as your friend comes running over to lunge onto the towel. Once your friend is in the hole, you can release your inhibitions and start laughing like a hyena!

Swapping Clothes

Ingredients
1 chest of drawers filled with clothes

While your friend or loved one is out, open up their chest of drawers and put the clothes in different drawers. Put the socks in the pants drawer; the underwear in the shirt drawer and so on. Let sit.

When your friend or loved one wakes up in the morning to get dress, they'll be confused and won't understand what happened to their clothes!

Air Freshener Grenade

Ingredients
1 air freshener aerosol can with a trigger
1 zip tie

In order for this prank to work, you need to find an aerosol can that has a "trigger" beneath the nozzle. Traditional aerosol cans with the "push trigger" will not work for this prank.

Find a room full of friends or family. Grab the aerosol can of air freshener in one hand and tie the zip tie loosely around the trigger with the other. Before tightening the zip tie, make sure that you've located the area where you want it to spray. One done, tighten the zip tie onto the nozzle and lob the object into the crowded room.

The aerosol can will start to spray out uncontrollably and will continue spraying until the contents have all been used up. The room will likely have to be quarantined for the rest of the day, as it will smell like a pine tree or wild strawberries.

Hidden Alarm Clocks

Ingredients
5 alarm clocks
1 bedroom

Set alarm clocks all to the same time, or a minute apart. Hide them in different portions of your friend's room. Hide one underneath the bed, another in the closet, one behind the computer or television, and let them all go off at the same time. Your victim won't know where the noises are coming from, since all of them will be sounding at the same time. But at least he'll thank you for letting him wake up that morning!

Locked in the Bathroom

Ingredients
1 door knob
1 bathroom
1 screw driver

This prank will take a bit of dedication and time, but it'll all be worth it in the end.

1. Use a screwdriver to remove the lock from the door. Once done, reverse the doorknob so that the locking mechanism is on the outside and the keyhole is on the inside. This switch will allow you to lock the person in the room from the outside.

For those who are mechanically inclined and think that the person inside might pick the lock from inside the bathroom, let it be known that there is also a way to block up the mechanism for the keyhole. A small BB or another obstruction can be used to block up the mechanism. But for this prank, I think that the old switcheroo will be good enough!

COMPUTER PRANKS

Timed Shutdown

Ingredients

1 computer running Windows

This prank will cause a timed shutdown whenever someone clicks on the shortcut to open their Internet browser.

Delete the shortcut for the user's Internet browser (i.e. Google Chrome, Firefox, Opera or Internet Explorer). Right click on the desktop, scroll down to the `New` tab and then select `Shortcut`. When a window pops up, don't select `Browse`. Instead, enter the following code into the text box: `shutdown -s -t 30`. The number "30" is the number of seconds that it will take for the computer to shutdown after the user has clicked on the shortcut. Click `Next`.

Right click on the shortcut on the desktop and select Rename. `Rename` the file the name of your friend or family member's Internet browser (i.e. Google Chrome, Internet Explorer, etc.) Once done, right click on the same shortcut and select `Properties`. A window will open. Once done, select `Change`

Icon on the bottom of the window and choose an icon that will disguise the shortcut as best as possible.

When your friend or family member goes to click on the shortcut, the computer will shut down in 30 seconds. It will continue to happen each time that they log on.

But remember, this prank is harmless, does no damage to the computer and can be resolved just by deleting the shortcut. Watch as they struggle to fix it!

Broken Windows

Ingredients
1 computer

This prank can be done either with the Windows or Mac OS operating systems.

While your friend or family member is out of the room, take a screen shot of their entire desktop. (In Windows, press the `PrtScrn` button and then open up Paint Shop and press `Ctrl+V`. In Mac OS X, press `Command+Shift+3`). Once the screen shot file has been saved, set it as the user's desktop background. Delete all of the shortcuts on their desktop.

This prank will give the user the illusion that all of their shortcuts are still on the screen, but, in reality, it's just an image of the shortcuts and none of them will be clickable. Watch from a distance as they struggle and laugh!

Annoying Homepage

Ingredients
1 computer

This prank can be done on Windows and Mac OS X operating systems. It's a simple prank to implement, but one that'll be sure to cause a stir.

In different Internet browsers, there are different ways to change the homepage. But I am going to instruct people how to do this with the Google Chrome browser. If your victim has another, then search Google for "change [browser name] homepage" and figure out how to do it.

Click on the only button in the upper right-hand corner. A menu bar will drop down. Select **Settings**. Under **Appearance**, check the **Show Home Button** radio button. The name of your current homepage will show up (i.e. www.google.com/) and next to it will be the high-lighted word **Change**. Click **Change**. In the prompt that comes up, change the URL in the text box to whatever you want your victim's new homepage to be. Something annoying would be preferable.

Once done, exit the browser. When your victim clicks on their Google Chrome shortcut, the browser will open up to the annoying Web site that you've now set as their homepage. And I'm sure if they're not too good with computers, they'll be begging you to change it!

The Broken Mouse

Ingredients
1 optical mouse
1 piece of Scotch tape

In order for this prank to work, your friend or family member must have an optical mouse (that is, the light on the bottom and not the scroll ball).

Carefully attach a piece of Scotch tape to the bottom of the mouse, so that the tape is covering the little light on the bottom. This will cause the mouse to not detect the surface and to not work. It'll cause your friend to scroll around like a madman for a minute before lifting the mouse and realizing that he's been pranked!

Flipping the Landscape

Ingredients

1 computer running Windows

In Windows, right click anywhere on the desktop and, when the menu comes up, click on `Screen Resolution`. A window will pop up. On the third bar to the bottom, click on the drop-down menu next to the word `Orientation` and select `Landscape (flipped)`.

If you're not too familiar with computers, this one might not make sense in the beginning. But just give it a try and see what happens: It'll become immediately clear how annoying it is.

Confusing Keys

Ingredients
1 computer running Windows

This prank can be maddening, but rest assured: It's a simple one to reverse and one that'll make for good laughs.

Click on the `Start` button (or Windows button) in the lower left-hand corner of your screen. Select `Control Panel`. Click on the `Clock, Region and Language` tab (on some versions of Windows, it's just called `Region and Language`). Select `Change keyboard or other input methods`. This will cause a window to pop up. Click on the button `Change keyboards...` and then click on the `Add...` button on the right-side of the window. Scroll down to `English (United States)` and select `United States-Dvorak`. Once done, click `OK` and exit the window.

And now, the text time that your friend goes to use his computer, he'll find that his words are all jumbled. Once again, this is an easy prank to reverse, but one that is well worth your time!

Farting in Error

Ingredients
1 computer running Windows

This prank can be done both on the Windows and Mac OS X operating systems, but, for the purpose of this book, I am going to list the instructions on how to do it on a Windows machine.

Click on the `Start` button (or Windows button) in the lower left-hand corner of your screen. Select `Control Panel`. Click on the `Hardware and Sound` tab. Under Sound, select `Change system sounds`. This will cause a window to pop up and it will list all of the actions and different sounds associated with different actions (for example, when an error message pops up, a certain sound will be made). To change the sounds, click on one of them and then select `Browse`. (The ideal sound to find would be the noise of flatulence. I'm sure that an Internet search for this audio file will yield good results.) Once done, select the noise of your choice and set it as the sound for all error messages.

It might take quite some time to get a laugh out of this prank, but when you're sitting in the other room and hear a fart noise, it'll make for a great laugh!

Autocorrecting Prank

Ingredients
1 computer running Windows

This prank can be done on a number of different operating systems, but, once again, I am going to be providing you with the instructions on how to do it on a Windows machine.

Click the `Start` button (or Windows button) on the lower left-hand corner of your screen. Select `Microsoft Office Word`, since this is the program that we're going to be using.

Once the program has been opened, look for the `Options` menu on the upper left-hand corner of the screen (this menu can be located in different places, depending on the version of Word that you're using). Once opened, click on the `Proofing` tab on the left-hand side. On the top of the window, you'll see a button that says, `AutoCorrect Options`. Click on that button and a window will come up.

In the window, you will notice that there is a table on the bottom. The words in the left column are the ones that, if typed out, will be replaced by the ones in the right column. To add another one to the list, simply enter a commonly used word (i.e., "the," "house," etc.) in the text box beneath the word "Replace," and then type in the word or phrase that you want that to be replaced by (for example, "I am watching you!") in the text box beneath the word "With." Press Add.

When your friend or loved one types out the word "the" and "I am watching you" comes up instead, they'll likely run out of the room in horror and you'll be laughing like mad in the other room!

Paint It Black

Ingredients
1 computer running Windows

This is a simple prank and one that's probably best used on those who don't know too much about computers. It'll turn the entire screen into "High Contrast Mode," which means that everything on the screen that's normally white will be changed to black and vice versa. It basically inverts all of the colors on the screen.

In order to do this, press `Shift+Alt+PrtScrn`. Once done, a window will appear prompting you to confirm that you want to go ahead with the change. Press `OK`.

Once this simple process is done, the computer will be in High Contrast Mode and your unwitting friend will think that something's gone terribly wrong. A simple prank, but again, best implemented on the computer illiterate!

The Invisible Mouse

Ingredients
1 wireless mouse
1 wireless keyboard

This prank is best done on people who have a desktop PC rather than a notebook computer. It'll allow you to hide the wireless receiver much better and will ensure the success of the prank.

Plug the receiver of your wireless mouse and keyboard into the USB slots on the back of your friend's computer. Hide somewhere in the house or workplace and, as he is hard at work, type a letter or move the mouse every so often. It'll make him think that someone's hacked his computer.

When the gig is almost up, just type "I'm watching you" as well, to ease his mind. And finally, come out of the shadows and fess up, laughing.

Task Scheduling

Ingredients
1 computer running Windows

This is one of the more difficult Windows pranks to implement, but you figure it out, it'll be one that even the best computer wizards might not be able to fix (without your help, of course).

Click the Start button (or Windows button) on the lower left-hand corner of your screen. In the `Search programs and files` bar, enter the word, "`Task Scheduler`." Click on the icon for the program called Task Scheduler. This action will open up a window for the Task Scheduler program.

On the right-hand side of the Task Scheduler window, click on `Create Basic Task`. This action will cause yet another window to appear, prompting you to enter the Name and Description of your task.

The first step is to enter some information in the Name and Description text boxes and then, to click

Next. (No specific information needs to be entered.) Once done, make sure that the Daily radio button is selected and then click the Next button again. Then, select the time that you'd like for the task to start and for how many days you'd want it to recur. For the best results, click "Display a Message" and write something for your friend to see each day. (If you'd like this prank to be longer and more drawn-out, then select "Start Program" and have a certain program start up at a scheduled time.)

This is a prank that'll continue for many, many days and one that'll amount to a great deal of frustration for your friend. After a month or so, it might be time to tell him that it's a prank. Once that's done, open up Task Scheduler like a good friend and fix the problem. He'll be happy to see the message gone once and for all.

The Ever-Loading Cursor

Ingredients
1 computer running Windows

As we all know, our mouse cursors are usually arrows, and that means that our computers are running healthily and smoothly. Sometimes, however, when our computers are running slow, the cursor changes into a circle (and, in the olden days, it used to be an hourglass).

In order to make your friend think that his computer is always loading and that it's slowing down miserably, just change his cursor indefinitely into the loading cursor. It'll make him go mad.

Click on the `Start` button (or Windows button) in the lower left-hand corner of your screen. Select `Control Panel`. In the search bar on the upper right-hand corner, type in the word, "`mouse`." This action will display a number of results, but search for the result that says, "`Change how the mouse pointer looks`," and click on it.

Once done, a window will appear called `Mouse Properties`. Click the `Normal Select` arrow if it is not already selected and then click on the Browse button below. Another window will appear showing you the different cursors that you can select from. Select the image of the "busy" arrow and then click open. Once done, the folder window will close. In `Mouse Properties`, click `Apply` and then exit all windows. Violà!

You'll notice that the cursor has changed into the busy cursor. The next day at work, your friend will be maddened, thinking his computer has slowed down. From time to time, as your sipping on your coffee, you can look over at him and bask in his frustration. Enjoy!

Printed by Amazon Italia Logistica S.r.l.
Torrazza Piemonte (TO), Italy